Mice In Space

Starring Max and Matilda Mouse

Written and illustrated by Alex Stitt

alphakids

One night a big cat was chasing two little mice down the street.

3

4

So the mice climbed up
and went inside.

The big cat was following them.

There was a loud **bang**.
The space rocket took off.

Oh no!

9

10

Back at the space rocket base, bells were ringing.

With all those holes, it looks like cheese to me.

Cheese?

Yum! Maybe I'll go out and get some.

Oh, **no** you won't!

13

The space rocket crew went to the space rocket.